ALL
GALL
IS
DIVIDED

BY E. M. CIORAN

All Gall Is Divided
Anathemas and Admirations
Drawn and Quartered
History and Utopia
On the Heights of Despair
A Short History of Decay
Tears and Saints
The Temptation to Exist
The Trouble with Being Born

ALL
GALL
IS
DIVIDED

~

THE APHORISMS OF

E. M. CIORAN

~

Translated from the French and with an introduction by

Richard Howard

Foreword by Eugene Thacker

ARCADE PUBLISHING • NEW YORK

Copyright © 1952, 1980 by Editions Gallimard
English-language translation copyright © 1999 by Arcade Publishing, Inc.
Foreword by Eugene Thacker copyright © 2019 by Skyhorse Publishing, Inc.

Originally published in France under the title *Syllogismes de l'amertume* by
Editions Gallimard

Arcade Publishing books may be purchased in bulk at special discounts for
sales promotion, corporate gifts, fund-raising, or educational purposes. Special
editions can also be created to specifications. For details, contact the Special Sales
Department, Arcade Publishing, 307 West 36th Street, 11th Floor, New York, NY
10018 or arcade@skyhorsepublishing.com.

Arcade Publishing® is a registered trademark of Skyhorse Publishing, Inc.®,
a Delaware corporation.

Visit our website at www.arcadepub.com.

10 9 8 7 6 5 4 3

Library of Congress Cataloging-in-Publication Data is available on file.

Print ISBN: 978-1-948924-23-8
Ebook ISBN: 978-1-61145-746-9

Printed in China

CONTENTS

❧

Foreword by Eugene Thacker
vii

Translator's Note
xiii

Atrophy of Utterance
1

The Swindler of the Abyss
21

Time and Anemia
41

Occident
55

The Circus of Solitude
69

Religion
91

Love's Vitality
105

On Music
115

Vertigo of History
121

Where the Void Begins
135

Foreword

The motives that enable a person to write in today's world seem to be as variegated as the number of books that are published. In spite of this, we are also aware of various cultural traditions that either compel one to write, or that bear down on an individual, making the act of writing all but impossible. One writes for one's self, or one writes for others. One writes to express, or to communicate, or to document. One writes for "readers," be they real, imagined, or nonexistent (or not yet existent). Though it is continually being transformed by new technologies, writing today still bears vestiges of these traditions: the nineteenth-century preoccupation with the expression of a unique and singular self, the modern anxieties over the possibility of effective and persuasive communication, and our contemporary mania for writing as a module in a broader publicity, marketing, and branding apparatus.

Cioran's aphorisms present the case for another kind of writing, one that, while it acknowledges these motives for writing, also offers another perspective: writing as "writing against." This is writing under the sign of negation, writing as the form of futility, as a poetics of the null state. While the urge to express, communicate, and document implies a broadly human-centric endeavor (Do you understand how I feel? Have I made myself clear? Have events been adequately recorded?), this other kind of writing harbors within itself an inexhaustible misanthropy, a constant experiment in style that is strangely spurred on by a repudiation of humanity, a granular misanthropy that knows no limits, including the antagonism against the self: writing against one's self, writing against other people, against humanity in general, against the species, against life, against existence, until such writing again becomes writing against one's self, as a misfortunate exemplar of others, the species, life, existence.

All Gall Is Divided was published in 1952, a few years after Cioran's self-imposed exile from Romania and the publication of first book in French, *A Short History of Decay*. The French title, *Syllogismes d'Amerture*, is conceptually evocative but difficult to translate. Literally rendered as "Syllogisms of Bitterness" or perhaps "Syllogisms of Spite," the title combines the properly philosophical form of logic (deductive reasoning) with that most improper and unphilosophical of sentiments (spite, bitterness, acridity). The book itself is shorter, the writing more taut, the tone more acerbic. It looks ahead to Cioran's later works such as *The Trouble with Being Born* or *Drawn and Quartered*, but it also looks back to some of the influences that run deeply through nearly all of Cioran's writing: the incisive wit and sarcasm of French moralists such as Chamfort and Joubert, the despair, doubt, and melancholy of Pascal's *Pensées*, the iconoclasm and polystylistic tour-de-force of Nietzsche's last writings. *All Gall* is a kind of writing that assembles its own tradition, though, as Cioran himself notes, it tends to be more a tradition of outsiders, those awkward lurkers in the back rows of the circus of humanity, many of whom have since been drawn, quite unwillingly, into the canon of "literature" or "philosophy" or worse, "wisdom sayings."

Given the book's predilection towards misanthropy, writing becomes a kind of indictment—in the final instance, an indictment of writing itself as that most elevated of cultural gestures that serves as the alibi for the species-specific superiority of human beings. Here "philosophy" can only be in ruins, "literature" only in the fragment, and it is here that the aphorism becomes Cioran's preferred mode of "writing-against." At once highly constructed yet casually scribbled down, the aphorism in Cioran's hands comes to encompass all the contradictions, inconsistencies, hypocrisies, and humility of being human. In interviews given some years later, Cioran is by turns glib and serious when discussing the aphorism. An interviewer will ask him why he prefers writing aphorisms, and Cioran will reply: "Because I'm lazy. In order to write something well-formed, you have to be proactive. For myself, I was *born* in the fragment. . . . I'm a victim of my own ideas. All that I've written amounts to nothing more than attacking literature, attacking life, attacking God. What would be the point of writing something well-formed? To prove what?" (To which he adds, "One doesn't become a professor with aphorisms.")

For Cioran, the aphorism seems far from the condensed jewels of wisdom of a kōan or a mantra—or does it? Fatigue and laziness, casualness and apathy, irritability and impulsiveness, the unfoundedness of the aphorism seems to strangely sit side-by-side with its rigorous construction, the negative approach to writing that consists in cross-out, erasing, deleting, what Cioran calls "that fear of collapsing with all the words." And, in its starkest moments, what follows for the writing seems to follow for the writer as well. One of the book's more harrowing lines reads: "without the idea of suicide, I'd have killed myself right away."

And yet, nowadays even misanthropy is said to have its part to play, as the shifting climates and diminishing resources of an indelibly human-centric planet continue to lurch onward with all the blind determination of what once passed as "progress." Near the end of *All Gall*, Cioran writes: "To make our way from the caves to the salons required a considerable amount of time; will we take as long to cover the path back, or will we take shortcuts?" Should books like this bear the duty of being instructive, or therapeutic, or inspirational? Should they have something to say to "us," wherever or whenever we are? Cioran didn't seem to think so. But then again, he also wrote: "When we are a thousand miles away from poetry, we still participate in it by that sudden need to scream—the last stage of lyricism." Perhaps what Cioran's writing in *All Gall* does is to allow another aspect of the aphorism to show, one that applies as much to the individual as it does to the species: the aphorism as epitaph.

Eugene Thacker

Translator's Note

Cioran's second book in French, *Syllogismes d'Amerture* — which we have chosen to call *All Gall Is Divided* for reasons divulged below — was something of a corrective to his first work, *Précis de Décomposition (A Short History of Decay)*; that is, the French readership, as is so often the case, resisted the initial instance of an alien resonance, though one entirely intimate with that grand French tradition of epigrammatic intensity which flourished in the texts of the seventeenth- and eighteenth-century *moralistes*. The Romanian's *Précis* ("for a writer to change languages," he muttered, "is to write a love letter with a dictionary") languished on the French publisher Gallimard's shelves, and it was only years later, after these thousand *sentences* of manic humor, howls of pain, and a vestige of tears had appeared, that the earlier book found an audience *prepared* for its contradictions and discomforts. The alternation of paragraph and sentence, of essay and aphorism, has continued through the decades of Cioran's literary production till 1992 (*Anathemas and Admirations*), and it is a great comfort to his translator that this writer's true rhythm of prose forms can now be observed in its entirety.

"A wisdom broken" is Francis Bacon's phrase for the aphorism — the very word has *horizon* within it, a dividing-line between sky and earth, a separation observed . . . And there is a further identification to be heard in Eliot's line: "to be eaten, to be divided, to be drunk/among whispers": something subversive, something perilous, always, about the aphorism, from the pre-Socratics to Chazal. Yet it ought to be noted that for all its classical analogies with the French epigram as we encounter it in La Rochefoucauld, in Chamfort, in Valéry, Cioran's breviary of estrangement fulfills the tradition with a difference. For these *remarks* which refuse the comforts of expansion, of explanation, of exfoliation, are nonetheless a narrative, an autobiography even, at least a confession. Not since Nietzsche has any thinker revealed himself so drastically, not since Heraclitus has the necessity of *fragments* been so deliriously welcomed. Hence my punning title for the syllogisms of bitterness, the allusion to Caesar's partition of France and, finally, Cioran's dissection of that other gall, the acrimony, the wormwood, the effrontery which is the consequence of "being born," the one regrettable act.

It was from Samuel Beckett that we first heard of Cioran, whose "little blue light" the author of *How It Is* discerned in the antres vast of consciousness, glowing with a certain sweetness for all of what Cioran calls "amertume" and Baudelaire calls "spleen." With this early volume of aphorisms, all of Cioran's French works are now translated into English; there remain the *Cahiers*, that grand treasury and infernal machine of fifteen years' maceration, which Arcade projects for that future Cioran viewed so darkly. If we have world enough and time, Cioran's *Notebooks, 1957–1972,* will yet assume an English dress not so different, it is hoped, from their French device.

Richard Howard

Atrophy of Utterance

Educated by weaklings, idolators of stigmata, especially fragmentary ones, we belong to a clinical age when only cases count. We loiter over what a writer has left unspoken, what he might have said: unarticulated depths. If he leaves an oeuvre, if he is explicit, he has earned our oblivion.

Wizardry of the unrealized artist . . . , of a loser who lets his disappointments go, unable to make them bear fruit.

～

So many pages, so many books which afforded us feeling and which we reread to study the quality of their adverbs, their adjectival aplomb.

～

1

Something serious about stupidity which, oriented differently, might multiply the stock of our masterpieces.

∾

If it weren't for our doubts about ourselves, all skepticism would be dead letter, conventional anxiety, philosophical doctrine.

∾

As for "verities," who can lug them around any longer? We refuse to bear their weight, to be their accomplices or their dupes. I dream of a world in which one might die for a comma.

∾

How I love those second-order minds (Joubert, in particular) who out of delicacy lived in the shadow of other men's genius, fearing to have such a thing, rejecting their own!

∾

If Molière had given himself up to his abyss, Pascal — with his — would look like a journalist.

∾

2

Certainties have no style: a concern for well-chosen words is the attribute of those who cannot rest easy in a faith. Lacking solid support, they cling to words — semblances of reality; while the others, strong in their convictions, despise appearances and wallow in the comfort of improvisation.

≈

Beware of those who turn their backs on love, ambition, society. They will take their revenge for having *renounced* . . .

≈

The history of ideas is the history of the spite of certain solitaries.

≈

Plutarch, nowadays, would write the *Parallel Lives of Losers.*

≈

English Romanticism was a happy mixture of laudanum, exile, and tuberculosis; German

Romanticism, of alcohol, suicide, and the provinces.

~

Certain minds ought to have lived in a German town in the Romantic period. How easy it is to imagine a Gérard de Nerval in Tübingen or Heidelberg!

~

German endurance knows no limits — even in madness: Nietzsche endured his eleven years, Hölderlin forty.

~

Luther, that prefiguration of modern man, assumed every kind of disequilibrium: both a Pascal and a Hitler cohabited within him.

~

"... only what is true is lovable..." — from this celebrated dictum derive the lacunae of France, her rejection of the Vague and the Indeterminate, her anti-poetry, her anti-metaphysics.

Even more than Descartes, Boileau was to weigh upon a whole nation and to censure its genius.

~

Hell — as precise as a ticket for a traffic violation;

Purgatory — false as all allusions to Heaven;

Paradise — window dressing of fictions and vapidity . . .

Dante's trilogy constitutes the highest rehabilitation of the Devil ever undertaken by a Christian.

~

Shakespeare: the rose and the ax have a rendezvous.

~

Default on your life and you accede to poetry — without the prop of talent.

~

Only superficial minds approach an idea with delicacy.

～

Mention of administrative rebuffs ("the law's delay, the insolence of office") among the justifications for suicide seems to me Hamlet's profoundest utterance.

～

When modes of expression are worn out, art tends toward non-sense, toward a private and incommunicable universe. An *intelligible* shudder, whether in painting, in music, or in poetry, strikes us, and rightly, as vulgar or out-of-date. The *public* will soon disappear; art will follow shortly.

A civilization which began with the cathedrals has to end with the hermeticism of schizophrenia.

～

When we are a thousand miles away from poetry, we still participate in it by that sudden need to scream — the last stage of lyricism.

～

To be a Raskolnikov — without the excuse of murder.

≈

The aphorism is cultivated only by those who have known fear *in the midst of words*, that fear of collapsing *with all the words*.

≈

If only we could return to those ages when no utterance shackled existence, to the laconism of interjections, to the joyous stupor of the pre-verbal!

≈

How easy it is to be "deep": all you have to do is let yourself sink into your own flaws.

≈

Every word affords me pain. Yet how sweet it would be if I could hear what the flowers have to say about death!

≈

Models of style: the swearword, the telegram, the epitaph.

~

The Romantics were the last specialists in suicide, which has been a shambles ever since. To improve its quality, we desperately need a new *mal de siècle*.

~

To cleanse literature of its greasepaint, to see its real countenance, is as dangerous as to dispossess philosophy of its jargon. Do the mind's creations come down to the transfiguration of trifles? Is there some sort of substance only *beyond words* — in catalepsy or the skull's grin?

~

The book which, after demolishing everything, fails to demolish itself will have exasperated us to no purpose.

~

Dislocated monads, here we are at the end of our prudent mopes, our well-planned anomalies: more than one sign heralds the hegemony of delirium.

∽

A writer's "sources"? His shames; failing to discover these in yourself, or dodging them when you do, you are doomed to plagiarism or reviewing.

∽

Every tormented "Occidental" suggests a Dostoyevskian hero with a bank account.

∽

The good dramaturge must have a talent for homicide; since the Elizabethans, who knows how to kill off his characters?

∽

The nerve cell is so used to everything, to anything, that we must despair of ever conceiving an insanity which — penetrating the brain — would make it explode.

∽

No one since Benjamin Constant has rediscovered the *tone* of disappointment.

∾

Supposing you have appropriated the rudiments of misanthropy; if you want to go further, you must go to school to Swift: he will teach you how to give your scorn of men the intensity of neuralgia.

∾

With Baudelaire, physiology entered into poetry; with Nietzsche, into philosophy. By them, the troubles of the organs were raised to song, to concept. With health the one thing proscribed, it was incumbent upon them to afford disease a career.

∾

Mystery — a word we use to deceive others, to convince them we are "deeper" than they are.

∾

If Nietzsche, Proust, Baudelaire, or Rimbaud survive the fluctuations of fashions, they owe it to the disinterestedness of their cruelty, to their demonic surgery, to the generosity of their spleen. What makes a work last, what keeps it from dating, is its ferocity. A gratuitous assertion? Consider the prestige of the Gospels, that aggressive book, a venomous text if ever there was one.

~

The public hurls itself upon the authors called "human"; the public knows it has nothing to fear from them: halted, like their readers, halfway down the road, these authors propose compromises with the Impossible, a coherent vision of Chaos.

~

The pornographer's verbal slovenliness frequently results from an excess of modesty, from the shame of displaying his "soul" and especially of naming it: there is no more indecent word in any language.

~

That there should be a reality hidden behind appearances is, after all, quite possible; that language might render such a thing would be an absurd hope. So why burden yourself with one opinion rather than another — why recoil from the banal or the inconceivable, from the duty of saying and of writing anything at all? A modicum of wisdom would compel us to sustain all theses at once, in an eclecticism of smiling destruction.

∾

Fear of sterility leads the writer to produce beyond his resources and to add to the lies of experience so many others borrowed or forged. Under each "Complete Works" lies an impostor.

∾

The pessimist has to invent new reasons to exist every day: he is a victim of the "meaning" of life.

∾

Macbeth: a Stoic of crime, Marcus Aurelius with a dagger.

∾

Mind is the great profiteer of the body's defeats. It grows rich at the expense of the flesh it pillages, exulting in its victim's miseries; by such brigandage it lives. — Civilization owes its fortune to the exploits of a bandit.

~

"Talent" is the surest way of perverting everything, of falsifying things and fooling oneself into the bargain. *Real* existence belongs only to those whom nature has not overwhelmed with any gift. Hence, it would be difficult to imagine a more fallacious universe than the literary kind or a man more devoid of *reality* than the man of letters.

~

No salvation, save in the *imitation* of silence. But our loquacity is prenatal. A race of rhetoricians, of verbose spermatozoons, we are *chemically* linked to the Word.

~

Pursuit of the sign to the detriment of the signified; language considered as an end in itself, as a rival of "reality"; verbal mania, among the philosophers themselves; the need to renew oneself *on the level of appearances;* —

characteristics of a civilization in which syntax surpasses the absolute and the grammarian excels the sage.

~

Goethe, the complete artist, is our antipodes: an example for others. Alien to incompletion, that modern concept of perfection, he refused comprehension of others' dangers; as for his own, he assimilated them so well that he never suffered from them. His brilliant destiny discourages us; after having sifted him in vain in an attempt to discover sublime or sordid secrets, we give ourselves up to Rilke's phrase: "I have no organ for Goethe."

~

We cannot sufficiently blame the nineteenth century for having favored that breed of glossators, those reading machines, that deformation of the mind incarnated by the Professor — symbol of a civilization's decline, of the corruption of taste, of the supremacy of labor over whim.

To see everything from the outside, to systematize the ineffable, to consider nothing straight on, to inventory the views of others! . . .

All commentary on a work is bad or futile, for whatever is not direct is null.

There was a time when the professors chose to pursue theology. At least they had the excuse then of professing the absolute, of limiting themselves to God, whereas in our century nothing escapes their lethal competence.

∾

What distinguishes us from our predecessors is our offhandedness with regard to Mystery. We have even renamed it: thus was born the Absurd . . .

∾

Fraudulence of style: to give the usual melancholies an unaccustomed turn, to decorate our minor miseries, to costume the void, to exist *by the word*, by the phraseology of the sarcasm or the sigh!

∾

Incredible that the prospect of having a biographer has made no one renounce having a life.

∾

Naive enough to set off in pursuit of Truth, I had explored — to no avail — any number of disciplines. I was beginning to be confirmed in my skepticism when the notion occurred to me of consulting, as a last resort, Poetry: who knows? perhaps it would be profitable, perhaps it conceals beneath its arbitrary appearances some definitive revelation . . . Illusory recourse! Poetry had outstripped me in negation and cost me even my *uncertainties* . . .

~

Once you have *inhaled* Death, what desolation in the odors of the Word!

~

Defeat being the order of the day, it is natural that God should thereby benefit. Thanks to the snobs who pity or abuse Him, He enjoys a certain vogue. But how long will He still be *interesting?*

~

"He had talent; why does no one bother about him anymore? He's been forgotten."

"It's only fair: he failed to take precautions to be *mis*understood."

∾

Nothing desiccates a mind so much as its repugnance to conceive obscure ideas.

∾

What are the occupations of the sage? He resigns himself to seeing, to eating, etc. . . . , he accepts in spite of himself this "wound with nine openings," which is what the Bhagavad-Gita calls the body. — Wisdom? To undergo with dignity the humiliation inflicted upon us by our holes.

∾

The poet: a sly devil who can torment himself at will, unearthing perplexities, obtaining them by every possible means. And afterward, naive posterity commiserates with him . . .

∾

Almost all works are made with flashes of imitation, with studied shudders and stolen ecstasies.

∾

Prolix in essence, literature lives on the plethora of utterance, on cancer of the word.

≈

Europe does not yet afford ruins enough for the epic to flourish. Yet everything suggests that, jealous of Troy and ready to imitate its fate, she will soon furnish themes so important that fiction and poetry will no longer suffice . . .

≈

Had he not held onto one last illusion, I would gladly ally myself with Omar Khayyam, with his unanswerable melancholy; but he still *believed* in wine.

≈

The best of myself, that point of light which distances me from everything, I owe to my infrequent encounters with a few bitter fools, a few disconsolate bastards, who, victims of the rigor of their cynicism, could no longer attach themselves to any vice.

≈

Before being a fundamental mistake, life is a failure of taste which neither death nor even poetry succeeds in correcting.

~

In this "great dormitory," as one Taoist text calls the universe, nightmare is the sole mode of lucidity.

~

Do not apply yourself to Letters if, with an obscure soul, you are haunted by clarity. You will leave behind you nothing but intelligible sighs, wretched fragments of your refusal to be yourself.

~

In the torments of the intellect, there is a certain bearing which is to be sought in vain among those of the heart.
Skepticism is the elegance of anxiety.

~

To be *modern* is to tinker with the Incurable.

~

Tragicomedy of the Disciple: I have reduced my mind to dust, in order to improve on the moralists who had taught me only to fritter it away . . .

The Swindler of the Abyss

Every thought should recall the ruin of a smile.

~

With infinite precaution, I prowl around the depths, draw off certain delirium, and make myself scarce, like a swindler of the Abyss.

~

Every thinker, at the start of his career, opts in spite of himself for dialectic or for weeping willows.

~

Long before physics and psychology were born, pain disintegrated matter, and affliction the soul.

~

That uncertain feeling when we try to imagine the daily life of great minds . . . Whatever could it be that Socrates was doing around two in the afternoon?

~

If we believe, so ingenuously, in ideas, it is because we forget that they were conceived by mammals.

~

A poetry worthy of that name begins with the experience of fatality. It is only the bad poets who are *free*.

~

In all the edifice of thought, I have found no category on which to rest my head. Whereas Chaos — there's a pillow!

~

To punish others for being happier than ourselves, we inoculate them — lacking anything better — with our anxieties. For our pains, alas! are not contagious.

~

Nothing slakes my thirst for doubts: if only I had Moses's staff to summon them from the very rock!

~

Except for the dilation of self, that fruit of total paralysis, what remedy for crises of annihilation, asphyxiation in the void, the horror of being no more than a soul in a gob of spit?

~

If melancholy has vouchsafed me such a dearth of ideas, that's because I loved it too much to let my mind deplete it.

~

A philosophical vogue is as irresistible as a gastronomic one: an idea is no better refuted than a sauce.

~

Every aspect of thought has its *moment*, its frivolity: in our time, the notion of Nothingness . . . How dated seem Matter, Energy, Spirit! Fortunately the lexicon is rich: each generation can delve there and come up with a word as important as the others — uselessly defunct.

~

We are all humbugs: we *survive* our problems.

~

In the days when the Devil flourished, panics, terrors, troubles were evils profiting from supernatural protection: we know who provoked them, who presided over their efflorescence; abandoned to themselves now, they become "internal dramas" or degenerate into "psychoses," a secularized pathology.

~

By compelling us to smile turn and turn about at the ideas of those we importune, Poverty degrades our skepticism into a livelihood.

~

The plant is mildly affected; the animal contrives to break down; in man the anomaly of all that breathes is exacerbated.

Life! homogeny of stupor and chemistry . . . Shall we take refuge in the equilibrium of the mineral kingdom? Step backward over the realm dividing us from it and imitate *normal* stone?

~

As far back as I can remember, I've utterly destroyed within myself the pride of being human. And I saunter to the periphery of the Race like a timorous monster, lacking the energy to claim kinship with some other band of apes.

~

Boredom levels all enigmas: a *positivist* reverie.

~

There is an *innate anxiety* which supplants in us both knowledge and intuition.

~

Death reaches so far, requires so much room, that I no longer know *where* to die.

~

Lucidity's task: to attain to a *correct* despair, an Olympian ferocity.

~

Happiness is so rare because we accede to it only *after* old age, in senility — a favor bestowed on very few mortals.

~

Our vacillations bear the mark of our probity; our assurances, of our imposture. A thinker's untruthfulness may be recognized by the sum of *precise* ideas he advances.

~

I plunged into the Absolute a fool; I emerged from it a troglodyte.

~

The cynicism of utter solitude is a calvary relieved by insolence.

~

Death poses a problem which replaces all the others. What is deadlier to philosophy, to the naive belief in the hierarchy of perplexities?

~

Philosophy offers an antidote to melancholy. And many still believe in the *depth* of philosophy!

~

In this provisional universe, our axioms have only the value of a *fait-divers*.

~

Anxiety was already a common product of the caveman. Imagine our Neanderthal's smile had he discovered that philosophers would one day claim to have invented it.

~

Philosophy's error is to be too *endurable*.

~

The abulic, leaving ideas alone, should be the only one given access to them. When men of action deal with ideas, our sweet quotidian clutter is organized into tragedy.

~

The advantage of meditating upon life and death is being able to say anything at all about them.

~

The Skeptic is perfectly willing to suffer, like other men, for life-giving chimeras. He fails to do so: a martyr of *common sense*.

~

Objection to scientific knowledge: this world doesn't *deserve* to be known.

~

How can a man be a philosopher? How can he have the effrontery to contend with time, with beauty, with God, and the rest? The mind swells and hops, shamelessly. Metaphysics, poetry — a flea's impertinences ...

∼

Stoicism for show: to be an enthusiast of *nil admirari*, an hysteric of ataraxia.

∼

If I can struggle against a fit of depression, in the name of what vitality can I oppose an obsession which belongs to me, which *precedes* me? In good health, I take the path I prefer; "sick," it is no longer I who decide: it is my disease. For the obsessed, no choice: their obsession has already opted for them, ahead of them. One chooses *oneself* when one possesses indifferent potentialities; but the distinctness of a disease antedates the diversity of the roads open to choice. To wonder if one is free or not — a trifle for a mind swept on by the calories of its deliriums. For such a mind, to extol freedom is to parade a discreditable health.

Freedom? Sophistry of *the fit*.

∼

Not content with real sufferings, the anxious man imposes imaginary ones on himself; he is a being for whom unreality exists, must exist; otherwise where would he obtain the ration of torments his nature demands?

～

Why not compare myself to the greatest saints? Have I expended less madness in order to safeguard my contradictions than they to surmount theirs?

～

When the Idea sought a refuge, it must have been decrepit, since it has found only the mind's hospitality.

～

A technique we practice at our cost, psychoanalysis degrades our risks, our dangers, our depths; it strips us of our impurities, of all that made us curious about ourselves.

～

Whether or not there exists a solution to problems troubles only a minority; that the emotions have no outcome, lead to nothing, vanish into themselves — that is the great unconscious drama, the *affective insolubility* everyone suffers without even thinking about it.

~

We undermine any idea by entertaining it *exhaustively;* we rob it of charm, even of life . . .

~

A little more fervor in my nihilism and I might — gainsaying *everything* — shake off my doubts and triumph over them. But I have only the taste of negation, not its grace.

~

Having experienced the fascination of extremes, and having stopped somewhere between dilettantism and dynamite!

~

31

It is the Intolerable, and not Evolution, which ought to be biology's hobbyhorse.

~

My cosmogony adds to primordial chaos an infinity of *suspension points* . . .

~

With every idea born in us, something in us rots.

~

Every problem profanes a mystery; in its turn, the problem is profaned by its solution.

~

Pathos betrays an abyss of bad taste; like that prurience of sedition in which a Luther, a Rousseau, a Beethoven, a Nietzsche indulged. The *grand accents* — plebeianism of solitaries.

~

That need for remorse which precedes wrongdoing, which actually creates it . . .

∾

Could I bear a single day without that charity of my madness which promises me the Last Judgment tomorrow?

∾

We suffer: the external world begins to exist . . . ; we suffer to excess: it vanishes. Pain instigates the world only to unmask its unreality.

∾

Thought which liberates itself from all prejudice disintegrates, imitating the scattered incoherence of the very things it would apprehend. With "fluid" ideas we *spread ourselves* over reality, we espouse it; we do not explicate it. Thus we pay dearly for the "system" we have not sought.

∾

The Real gives me asthma.

∾

33

We dislike following, or leading, to its conclusion a depressing train of thought, however unassailable; we resist it just when it affects our entrails, at the point where it becomes *malaise*, truth and disaster of the flesh. — No sermon of the Buddha, no page of Schopenhauer fails to turn my stomach . . .

∽

Subtlety is encountered:

among theologians. Unable to prove what they propose, they are obliged to practice so many distinctions that they distract the brain; their purpose. Imagine the virtuosity required to classify angels into ten or a dozen species! Not to mention God: how many minds has His exhausting "infinity" cast into deliquescence;

among the idle — among the worldly, the nonchalant, among all who feed on words. Conversation — mother of subtlety . . . Insensitive to it, the Germans have been swallowed up by metaphysics. But the talkative peoples, the ancient Greeks and the French, inured to the graces of the mind, have excelled in the *technique of trifles;*

among the persecuted. Liable to lying, to ruse and machination, they lead a double life, a false one: *insincerity* — out of need — excites the intelligence. Sure of themselves, the English are boring; thus they pay for the centuries of liberty during which they could live without recourse to cunning, to the sly smile, to *expedients*. Easy to understand why, diametrically opposite, it is the Jews' privilege to be the most wide-awake of peoples;

among women. Condemned to modesty, they must camouflage their desires and lie: *lying is a form of talent*, whereas respect for the "truth" goes along with heaviness and vulgarity;

among the criminal — who are not confined . . . , among those for whom one might conceive an ideal penal code.

～

Still young, we launch ourselves into philosophy, searching not so much for a vision as for a stimulant; we track down ideas, diagnose the delirium which has produced them, dreaming of imitating and exaggerating it. Adolescence delights in the juggling act of altitudes; what it loves in a thinker is the acrobat; in Nietzsche, we loved Zarathustra, his poses, his mystical clown-show, a real *farmer's market of the peaks* . . .

His idolatry of power derives not so much from an evolutionist snobbery as from an inner tension he has projected outward, from an intoxication which interprets becoming and accepts it. A false image of life and of history was the result. But we had to pass through such things, through the philosophical orgy, the cult of vitality. Those who refused to do so will never know the relapse, the antipodes and the grimaces of this cult; they will remain closed off from the sources of disappointment.

We had believed with Nietzsche in the perpetuity of trances; thanks to the maturity of our cynicism, we have ventured further than he. The notion of the superman now strikes us as no more than a lucubration; it used to seem as precise as a *given* of experience. Thus the enchanter of our youth fades. But *which one* of him — if he was *several* — still remains? It is the expert in failures, the *psychologist*, an aggressive psychologist, not merely an observer like the moralists. He scans with the eye of an enemy and makes enemies for himself. But he draws such enemies out of himself, like the vices he denounces. Does he attack the weak? He is merely being introspective; and when he attacks decadence, he is describing his condition. All his hatreds bear indirectly on himself. His weaknesses he proclaims and erects into an ideal; if he execrates himself, Christianity or socialism suffers for it. His diagnosis of nihilism is irrefutable: because he himself is a nihilist, and because he avows it. A pamphleteer in love with his adversaries, he could not have endured himself had he not done battle with himself, against himself — had he not placed his miseries elsewhere, in the others: *on them he took revenge for what he was.* Having practiced psychology as a hero, he proposed to the enthusiasts of the Inextricable a diversity of stalemates.

We measure his fecundity by the possibilities he affords us of continually repudiating him without exhausting him. A nomad mind, he is good at varying his disequilibriums. In all matters, he has championed the *pro* and the *con:* this is the procedure of those who give themselves up to speculation for lack of being able to write tragedies — to disperse themselves in many destinies. Nonetheless, by exhibiting his hysterias, Nietzsche has spared us the shame of ours; his miseries were salutary for us. He has opened *the age of "complexes."*

≈

The "generous" philosopher forgets to his cost that in any system only the detrimental truths survive.

≈

At the age when, for lack of experience, one takes to philosophy, I determined to write a thesis like everyone else. What subject to choose? I wanted one that would be both familiar and unwonted. The moment I imagined I had found it, I hastened to announce my discovery to my professor.

"What would you think of *A General Theory of Tears*? I feel ready to start work on that."

"Possibly," he said, "but you'll have your work cut out, finding a bibliography."

"That doesn't matter so much. All History will afford me its authority," I replied in a tone of triumphant impertinence.

But when, in his impatience, he shot me a glance of disdain, I resolved then and there to murder *the disciple* in myself.

∾

In other times, the philosopher who did not write but thought incurred no scorn thereby; ever since we began prostrating ourselves before the effective, *the work* has become the absolute of vulgarity; those who produce none are regarded as failures. But such failures would have been the sages of another age; they will redeem ours by having left no traces.

∾

More than once it has occurred to me to glimpse the autumn of the mind, the denouement of consciousness, reason's final scene, then a light which froze my blood!

~

Toward a vegetal wisdom: I would abjure all my terrors for the smile of a tree . . .

Time and Anemia

How close she is to me, that old mad-woman running after time, trying to catch up with a *piece* of time!

～

A link exists between the deficiency of our blood and our embarrassment in duration: so many white globules, so many empty moments . . . Don't our conscious states derive from the discoloration of our desires?

～

Surprised at high noon by the delicious terror of dizziness, how to account for it?

Something in the blood? in the heavens? or in anemia, located halfway between?

~

Our pallor shows us to what degree the body can understand the soul.

~

You with your veins full of night — you have no more place among men than an epitaph in the middle of a circus.

~

At the climax of Incuriosity, you think of a good fit of epilepsy as if it were the promised land.

~

Your passion ruins you in direct proportion to the diffusion of its object; mine was Boredom: I have succumbed to its imprecision.

~

Time is denied me. Unable to follow its cadence, I clutch or contemplate it, but follow it?

never: it is not my *element*. And it is in vain that I crave a little of *everyone's* time!

~

Leukemia is the garden where God blooms.

~

If faith, politics, or bestiality alleviates despair, everything leaves melancholy intact: it can cease only with our blood.

~

Boredom is a larval anxiety; depression, a dreamy hatred.

~

Our sadnesses prolong the mystery sketched by the mummies' smile.

~

Black utopia, anxiety alone affords us *exact details* about the future.

~

Vomit? Pray? — Boredom makes us climb to a heaven of Crucifixion which leaves in our mouths a saccharine aftertaste.

~

For a long time I believed in the metaphysical virtues of Fatigue: true, it drags us down to the roots of Time; but what do we bring back? Some twaddle about eternity.

~

"I am like a broken puppet whose eyes have fallen inside." This remark of a mental patient weighs more heavily than a whole stack of works of introspection.

~

When everything stales around us, how tonic our curiosity to know *how* we lose our reason!

~

If only we could abandon at will the nothingness of apathy for the dynamism of remorse!

~

Compared to the kind that lies ahead of me, the boredom inhabiting me now seems so gratifyingly intolerable that I dread consuming its terrors.

~

In a world without melancholy, nightingales would belch.

~

If someone incessantly drops the word "life," you know he's a sick man.

~

We are interested in Time because we are snobs of the Irreparable.

~

How long does it take to be initiated into depression, cottage industry of the Vague? Some require only a second, others a lifetime.

~

Many times I have sought refuge in that lumber room which is Heaven, many times I have yielded to the need to *suffocate* in God!

~

I am myself only above or beneath myself, in rage or prostration; on my habitual level, I am unaware that I exist.

~

It is not easy to acquire a neurosis; should you succeed, you possess a fortune which everything favors: victories as well as defeats.

~

We can function only with regard to a limited duration: a day, a week, a month, a year, ten years, or a lifetime. But if, by mischance, we refer our actions to Time, time and actions evaporate: that is the venture into the Void, the genesis of the Negative.

~

Sooner or later, each desire must encounter its lassitude: its truth . . .

~

Awareness of time: assault on time . . .

~

Thanks to depression — that alpinism of the indolent — we scale every summit and daydream over every precipice *from our bed*.

~

To be bored is to guzzle time.

~

The armchair, with so much to answer for, that promoter of our "soul."

~

Erect I make a resolution; *prone* I revoke it.

~

How easily one would accommodate oneself to sorrows if one's reason or one's liver did not succumb to them.

~

I've sought my own model within myself. As for imitating it, I've relied on the dialectic of indolence. It is so much pleasanter not to accomplish oneself!

~

47

To have devoted to the idea of death all the hours which any vocation demands . . . Metaphysical outbursts are the attribute of monks, debauchees, and bums. A job would have turned Buddha into a mere *malcontent*.

~

Compel men to lie down for days on end: couches would succeed where wars and slogans have failed. For the operations of Ennui exceed in effectiveness those of weapons and ideologies.

~

Our disgusts? — Detours of the disgust with ourselves.

~

When I catch myself nursing an impulse to Revolt, I take a sleeping pill or consult a psychiatrist. Any means will do if you pursue Indifference without being predisposed to it.

~

Premise of idlers, those born metaphysicians, the Void is the certainty discovered — at the end of their career, and as a reward for their disappointments — by honest people and professional philosophers.

~

In proportion as we liquidate our shames, we discard our masks. The day comes when the game ends: no more shames, no more masks. And no more *public*. — We have presumed too much on our secrets, on the vitality of our woes.

~

I have daily converse with my skeleton — something my flesh will never forgive.

~

What spoils joy is its lack of rigor; on the other hand, just consider the logic of gall.

~

If just once you were depressed *for no reason*, you have been so all your life without knowing it.

~

I gallivant through the days like a prostitute in a world without sidewalks.

~

You side with life only when you utter — *with all your heart* — a banality.

~

Between Ennui and Ecstasy unwinds our whole experience of time.

~

Has your life amounted to something? — You will never know *pride*.

~

We take refuge behind our countenance; the madman is betrayed by his. He offers himself, denounces himself to others. Having lost his mask, he publishes his anguish, imposes it on the first comer, parades his enigmas. So much indiscretion is irritating ... It is only natural that we consign him to strait jackets and isolation wards.

~

Any and all water is the color of drowning.

≈

Call it insensitivity or a passion for remorse, I have never undertaken to rescue what little Absolute this world contains.

≈

Becoming: an agony *without an ending*.

≈

Unlike pleasures, pains do not lead to satiety. There is no blasé leper.

≈

Melancholy: an appetite no misery satisfies.

≈

Nothing flatters us so much as an obsession with death; the *obsession*, not death.

≈

Those hours when it seems futile to get up sharpen my curiosity about the Incurable. Nailed to their beds, and to the Absolute, how much they must know about everything! But I approach them by no more than the virtuosities of torpor, the ruminations of a lazy morning.

≈

As long as boredom is confined to affairs of the heart, everything is still possible; once it spreads into the sphere of judgment, we are done for.

≈

We rarely meditate in a standing position, still less walking. It is from our insistence on maintaining the vertical that Action is born; hence, to protest its misdeeds, we ought to imitate the posture of corpses.

≈

Despair is misery's flaunt, a form of provocation, a philosophy for indiscreet epochs.

≈

52

We no longer dread tomorrow once we learn to take Nothingness into our arms. Boredom works wonders: it converts vacuity into substance, it is itself a fostering void.

~

The older I grow, the less I enjoy performing my little Hamlet. Already I no longer know, with regard to death, which torment to try . . .

Occident

Modern pride: I have lost the friendship of a man I esteemed, having insistently reminded him I was more degenerate than he.

∼

In vain the West seeks a form of final agony worthy of its past.

∼

Don Quixote represents a civilization's youth: he *made up* events; — and we don't know how to escape those besetting us.

∼

The East has consulted flowers and renunciation. Our response? Machines and effort, and that galloping melancholy — the West's last spasm.

≈

How sad to see great nations begging for a little extra future!

≈

Our epoch will be marked by the romanticism of the stateless. Already apparent is the image of a universe in which no one will have *droit de cité*.

Inside every citizen nowadays lies a future alien.

≈

A millennium of warfare consolidated the West; a century of "psychology" has ripped it to tatters.

≈

By means of sects, the mob participates in the Absolute, and a nation manifests its vitality. It was sects, in Russia, which prepared the revolution, the Slavic deluge.

Once Catholicism offered its splendid

rigor, sclerosis set in; yet its career is not over: it can still wear mourning for Latinity.

~

Our disease being history's, the disease of history's eclipse, we must fall back on Valéry's remark, must exacerbate its bearing: we know, now, that *all* civilization is mortal, that we are hurtling toward horizons of apoplexy, toward the miracles of the worst, toward the golden age of terror.

~

By the intensity of its conflicts, the sixteenth century is closer to us than any other; yet I see no Luther, no Calvin in our time. Compared to those giants, and to their contemporaries, we are pygmies promoted, by the fatality of knowledge, to a monumental destiny. — If we lack style, we nonetheless score one point over them: in all their tribulations they had the excuse, the cowardice, of counting themselves among the elect. For them Predestination, the one still-tempting Christian idea, retained its double face. For us, there are no more *elect*.

~

Listen to Germans and Spaniards *explain themselves;* your ears will be ringing with the same old refrain: tragic, tragic . . . It is their way of making you understand their calamities or their stagnations, their style of success . . .

Now turn to the Balkans; in every sentence you will hear: destiny, destiny . . . By which certain peoples, too close to their origins, camouflage their ineffectual depressions. It is the discretion of troglodytes.

~

From contact with the French, one learns to be unhappy *politely.*

~

The nations which lack the taste for dalliance, for frivolity and approximation, which *live* their verbal exaggerations, are a catastrophe for the others — and for themselves. They lay stress on bagatelles, inject seriousness into the accessory and tragedy into trifles. Because they are still encumbered with a passion for fidelity and with a hateful repugnance to betrayal, there is nothing more to be hoped from them, save their ruin. In order to correct their merits, to remedy their depths, they must be converted to

the South and be inoculated with the virus of
Farce.

~

Had Napoleon occupied Germany with
the citizens of Marseilles, the face of the world
would be altogether different.

~

Might the solemn nations be meridional-
ized? The future of Europe hangs on this question.
If the Germans return to their labors as before, the
West is doomed; similarly if the Russians fail to
recover their old love of sloth. With the former as
with the latter, we must encourage a taste for the
farniente, for apathy and siesta, luring them both
with the delights of versatility and decay.

. . . Otherwise be resigned to the solutions
which Prussia, or Siberia, will inflict upon our
dilettantism.

~

There is no enthusiasm and no evolution
which fail to be destructive, at least at their
moments of intensity.

~

Heraclitus defies time with his *becoming;* Bergson's joins the gullible experiments, philosophy's old toys.

~

Happy those monks who, late in the Middle Ages, ran from town to town announcing the end of the world! Was the fulfillment of their prophecies . . . delayed? At least they could vent their passions, give free rein to their terrors, releasing them upon the crowd; — illusory therapeutics in an age like ours, when panic, now among our mores, has lost its virtues.

~

To control men, you must practice their vices and add to them. Consider the popes: as long as they fornicated, gave themselves up to incest and murder, they ruled their age; and the church was omnipotent. No sooner did they respect its precepts than they declined, and still do: abstinence, like moderation, has been fatal to them; now that they're respectable, who fears them? Edifying twilight of an institution.

~

A prejudice in favor of honor is the feature of a rudimentary civilization. It vanishes with the advent of lucidity, with the regime of cowards, of those who, having "understood" everything, have nothing left to defend.

~

For three centuries, Spain jealously guarded the secret of Ineffectuality; today this secret is possessed by all Western nations; they have not filched it, they have discovered it by their own efforts, *by introspection.*

~

By barbarity, Hitler attempted to save an entire civilization. His enterprise was a failure; — it was nonetheless the West's last *initiative.*

No doubt Europe deserved something better. Who is to blame if it could not produce a higher-quality monster?

~

Rousseau was a scourge for France, comparable to Hegel for Germany. As indifferent to hysteria as to systems, England has come to terms with mediocrity; her "philosophy" has established the value of *sensation;* her politics, that of *the affair.* Empiricism was her answer to the Continent's lucubrations; Parliament, her challenge to Utopia, to all heroic pathologies.

No political equilibrium without first-rate nonentities. Who provokes catastrophes? Those possessed by restlessness, the impotent, the insomniacs, the failed artists who have worn a crown, a uniform, or a saber, and, worst of all, the optimists, those who *hope* on others' backs.

～

There is a lack of elegance in overdoing bad luck; certain individuals, like certain nations, indulge in it so deeply that they dishonor tragedy.

～

Lucid minds, in order to give an official character to their lassitude and impose it upon others, ought to constitute themselves into a *League of Disappointment.* Thereby they might succeed in attenuating the pressure of history, in rendering history optional.

～

Be that as it may, I have worshiped and abhorred numerous nations; — it has never entered my mind to deny the Spaniard I'd have loved to be . . .

∾

I — Vacillating instincts, corroded beliefs, obsessions, and anility: everywhere conquerors in retreat, *rentiers* of heroism confronting the young Alarics who lie in wait for Rome and Athens; everywhere paradoxes of the lymphatic. There was a time when salon sallies traversed whole countries, foiled stupidity or refined it. Europe, coquettish and intractable, was in the flower of her age; — decrepit today, Europe excites no one. Even so, certain barbarians await their chance to inherit the finery, impatient at her long agony.

II — France, England, Germany; Italy perhaps. The rest . . . By what accident does a civilization stop? Why did Dutch painting or Spanish mysticism flourish only a moment? So many peoples who survive their own genius! Hence, their decline is tragic; but that of France, of Germany, and of England proceeds from an inner irreparability, from the completion of a process, from a task fulfilled; it is natural, explicable, deserved. Could it have been otherwise? These countries have prospered and have ruined themselves together, by a spirit of rivalry, of fraternity, and of hatred; yet, over the rest of the globe, the fresh rabble was storing up energies, multiplying, waiting . . .

Tribes with imperious instincts were agglutinating in order to form a great power; the moment comes when, resigned and ramshackle, they sigh for a subaltern role. When one no longer invades, one consents to be invaded. Hannibal's drama was to be born too soon; a few centuries later, he would have found Rome's gates open. The Empire was vacant, like Europe in our time.

III — We have all had a taste of the West's disease: art, love, religion, war — we know too much about them all to believe in them now; then too, so many centuries have worn them down . . . The epoch of the *finite* in plenitude is past; the substance of poems? Exhausted. — To love? Even the riffraff repudiates "sentiment." Piety? Search the cathedrals; only ineptitude kneels there now. Who still wants to do battle? The hero is out-of-date; only impersonal carnage holds sway. We are clairvoyant puppets, scarcely capable of performing our curtsies before the irremediable.

The West? A *potential* without a future.

IV — Unable to defend our wits against muscles, we shall be less and less fit for any purpose whatever: the first comer will bind us hand and foot. Contemplate the West: overflowing with knowledge, with dishonor, with phlegm. To this was to come the crusaders, the knights, the pirates: to the stupor of a *mission accomplished.*

When Rome called back her legions, she was unaware of History and the lessons of twilight. Such is not our case. What grim Messiah is about to fall upon us!

∾

Whether out of inadvertence or incompetence, he who however briefly halts humanity on its march is humanity's benefactor.

∾

Catholicism created Spain only the better to smother her: a country one travels to in order to admire the Church and to divine the pleasure that can be taken in murdering a priest.

∾

The West is making progress, timidly sporting its senility — and already I feel less envy of those who, having seen Rome founder, believed they were enjoying a unique and intransmissible desolation.

~

The truths of humanism, the confidence in mankind and all the rest, still possess only the vigor of fictions, only a prosperity of shadows. The West was these truths; it is no more than these fictions, these shadows. As helpless as they, it has not been given to the West to vivify them. It drags them along, exposes them, but no longer *imposes* them; they have ceased to be *threatening*. Hence, those who cling to humanism make use of an exhausted expression, without an affective support — a spectral substantive.

~

This continent of ours may not have played its last card after all. What if it were to set about demoralizing the rest of the world, spreading its corruptions there? — That would be, for Europe, a way of preserving its prestige a little longer, exerting its influence.

~

In the future, if humanity is to begin again, it will do so with its failures, with the Mongols of the entire globe, with the dregs of the continents; a parody civilization will appear which those who produced the real one will observe quite impotent, ashamed, prostrate, in order to take refuge, ultimately, in an idiocy where they will forget the glamour of their disasters.

The Circus of Solitude

I

You cannot protect your solitude if you cannot make yourself odious.

~

I live only because it is in my power to die when I choose to: without the *idea* of suicide, I'd have killed myself right away.

~

The skepticism which fails to contribute to the ruin of our health is merely an intellectual exercise.

~

To nourish in destitution a tyrant's bad temper; to seethe beneath a repressed cruelty; to loathe oneself for lack of subalterns to massacre, of an empire to terrorize; to be a needy Tiberius . . .

~

The irritating thing about despair is its obviousness, its visibility, its "documentation": what is it but reportage? Consider hope, on the contrary — its generosity in what is false, its mania for *affabulation*, its rejection of the event: an aberration, a fiction. And it is in this aberration that life resides and upon this fiction that it feeds.

~

Caesar? Don Quixote? Which of the two, in my presumption, would I take as a model? It makes no difference. The fact is that one day, in a far country, I set off to conquer the world, all the perplexities of the world . . .

~

Considering the city from an attic window, it seems to me quite as honorable to be a sacristan here as a pimp.

~

If I had to renounce my dilettantism, it is in howling that I would specialize.

~

You cease being young the moment you no longer choose your enemies, when you are content with those you have within arm's reach.

~

All our resentments derive from one circumstance: remaining beneath ourselves, we have been unable to get back up, to rejoin . . . This we shall never forgive *the others*.

~

Adrift in the Vague, I cling to each wisp of affliction as to a drowning man's plank.

~

To propagate disequilibrium, to aggravate mental disturbance, to construct sanatoriums on every street corner — forbid *swearing*.

Then you will comprehend its liberating virtues, its therapeutic function, the superiority of its method over that of psychoanalysis, of Eastern gymnastics or Catholic ones; you will understand, above all, that it is thanks to the wonders of swearing, to its constant aid at every moment that most of us have managed not to be criminals or lunatics.

~

We are born with such a capacity for admiration that ten other planets could scarcely exhaust it; — the earth manages in a trice.

~

To get up each morning as a thaumaturge determined to populate your day with miracles, and then to fall back into bed ruminating till dark the aggravations of love and money . . .

~

Contact with men has rubbed the bloom off my neuroses.

~

Nothing reveals the vulgar man better than his refusal to be disappointed.

~

When I haven't a penny in my pocket, I compel myself to imagine *the heaven of sounding light* which constitutes, according to Japanese Buddhism, one of the stages the wise man must pass through in order to overcome the world — and maybe money, I would add.

~

Of all calumnies the worst is the one which attacks our indolence, which contests its authenticity.

~

In my childhood, we boys played a game: we would watch the gravedigger at work. Sometimes he would hand us a skull, with which we would play soccer. For us that was a delight which no funereal thought came to darken.

For many years now, I have lived in a milieu of priests having to their credit many thousands of extreme unctions; yet I have not known a single one who was intrigued by Death. Later on I was to understand that the only corpse from which we can gain some advantage is the one *preparing itself* within us.

~

Without God, everything is nothingness; and God? Supreme nothingness.

II

The desire to die was my one and only concern; to it I have sacrificed everything, even death.

~

The moment an animal breaks down, it begins resembling a man. Just look at a rabid dog or an abulic one: as if it was awaiting its novelist or its poet.

~

Every profound experience is formulated in terms of physiology.

~

Flattery turns character into a puppet, and in an instant, under its sway, the liveliest eyes assume a bovine expression. Insinuating itself deeper than disease, and transforming to the

74

same degree our glands, our entrails, and our mind, flattery is the only weapon we possess to enslave our kind, to demoralize and to corrupt them.

~

Within the pessimist an ineffectual kindness connives with an unsatiated malice.

~

I have dispatched God out of a need for meditation, I have rid myself of a last nuisance.

~

The more misfortunes surround us, the more trivial we become; even our gait is changed. They invite us to show off, they smother our person in order to waken within us the *character*.

~

. . . Had it not been for the impertinence of supposing myself the most wretched being on earth, I should have collapsed long since.

~

What an insult to man, supposing that in order to destroy himself he needs a stimulus, a destiny . . . Has he not already expended the best of himself in liquidating his own legend? In this refusal to endure, in this horror of self abides his excuse or, as we used to say, his grandeur.

∿

Why abandon the game, when there remain so many for us to *disappoint?*

∿

When I am subject to the passions, to spasms of faith or intolerance, I would gladly go down into the street to fight and die as a partisan of the Vague, a fanatic of Perhaps . . .

∿

You have dreamed of setting the universe ablaze, and you have not even managed to communicate your fire to words, to *light up* a single one!

∿

Right in the middle of serious studies, I discovered that one day I would die . . . ; my modesty was shaken. Convinced that I had nothing left to learn, I abandoned my studies to inform the world of such a remarkable discovery.

∾

A positive spirit gone wrong, the Destroyer believes, in his candor, that truths are worth the trouble of being destroyed. He is a technician the wrong way around, a pedant of vandalism, a distracted evangelist.

∾

Aging, one learns to swap one's terrors for one's sneers.

∾

No longer ask me for my program: isn't *breathing* one?

∾

The best way of distancing ourselves from others is to invite them to delight in our defeats; afterward, we are sure to hate them for the rest of our days.

∾

"You must do some work, gain your livelihood, muster your strength."

"My strength? I've wasted my strength, used it all up erasing whatever traces of God I could find within myself . . . and now I'll be *unemployed* forever!"

∾

Every action flatters the hyena within us.

∾

At the nadir of our failures, we suddenly grasp the *essence* of death; — a limit-perception, refractory to expression; a metaphysical defeat which words cannot perpetuate. This explains why, on this theme, the interjections of an illiterate old woman enlighten us more than a philosopher's jargon.

∾

Nature has created individuals only to relieve Suffering, to help it spread and scatter at their expense.

∾

Whereas it takes the sensibility of a man flayed alive or a long tradition of vice in order to associate pleasure with the consciousness of pleasure, pain and the consciousness of pain are identified even in an imbecile.

~

To conjure away suffering, to degrade it into pleasure — hoax of introspection, wile of the delicate, diplomacy of the whimper.

~

Having so often changed attitudes with regard to the sun, I am no longer sure what footing we're on.

~

We discern a flavor in our days only when we dodge the obligation to have a destiny.

~

The more indifferent I am to men, the more they trouble me; and when I scorn them, I cannot approach them without stammering.

~

If we squeezed a madman's brain, the liquid that emerged would seem like honey compared to the gall secreted by certain melancholics.

~

No one should try to live if he has not completed his training as a victim.

~

Even more than a defense mechanism, timidity is a *technique*, constantly perfected by the megalomania of the misunderstood.

~

Not having had the luck to have alcoholic parents, one must intoxicate oneself one's whole life to make up for the heavy heredity of their virtues.

~

Can one speak honestly of anything except God or oneself?

III

The odor of the creature puts us on the track of a fetid divinity.

~

If History had a goal, how lamentable would be the fate of those of us who have accomplished nothing! But in the universal purposelessness, we stand proud, ineffectual streetwalkers, riffraff well-pleased with having been right.

~

What anxiety when one is not sure of one's doubts and wonders: are these actually doubts?

~

He who has not contradicted his instincts, who has not imposed upon himself a long period of sexual deprivation or has not known the depravities of abstinence, will be inaccessible to the language of crime and to that of ecstasy: he will never understand the obsessions of the Marquis de Sade nor those of Saint John of the Cross.

~

The merest subservience, even to the desire to die, unmasks our loyalty to the impostures of the self.

~

When you suffer the temptation of Good, go to the marketplace and out of the crowd choose an old, disinherited woman and step on her toes. You will stare at her outrage without answering so much as a word, so that she may finally know, thanks to the spasm afforded by the abuse of an adjective, a moment's glory.

~

What is the use of getting rid of God in order to fall back on yourself? What good this substitution of one carrion for another?

~

The beggar is a poor man who, impatient with adventures, has abandoned poverty in order to explore the jungles of pity.

~

We cannot avoid the defects of men without fleeing, thereby, their virtues. So we ruin ourselves by wisdom.

~

Without the hope of a greater pain, I could not endure the one of the moment, however infinite.

~

To hope is to *contradict* the future.

~

For all eternity, God has chosen everything for us, down to our neckties.

~

No action, no success without a total attention to *secondary* causes ... Life is an insect's occupation.

~

The tenacity I have deployed to combat the magic of suicide would have easily sufficed to achieve my salvation, to pulverize myself within God.

~

When nothing needles us further, "depression" is there, the last stimulant. No longer able to do without it, we pursue it in diversion as in prayer. And so greatly do we dread being deprived of it that "Give us this day our daily blues" becomes the refrain of our expectations, our entreaties.

~

However intimate we may be with the operations of the mind, we cannot *think* more than two or three minutes a day; — unless, by taste or profession, we practice, for hours on end, brutalizing words in order to extract ideas from them.

The *intellectual* represents the major disgrace, the culminating failure of Homo sapiens.

~

What gives me the illusion of never having been duped is that I have never loved anything without having thereby hated it.

~

However versed we may be in satiety, we remain caricatures of our precursor Xerxes. Was it not he who promised by edict a reward to anyone who could invent a new pleasure? — That was the most modern gesture of antiquity.

IV

The more *risks* a mind runs, the more it experiences the need to appear superficial, to assume an air of frivolity, and to multiply misunderstandings on its own account.

～

After thirty, one should be no more interested in events than an astronomer in gossip.

～

Only the idiot is equipped to breathe.

～

With age, it is not so much our intellectual faculties which diminish as that *power to despair* of which, in youth, we could appreciate neither the charm nor the absurdity.

∾

What a pity that to reach God we must pass through faith!

∾

Life — that *style pompier* of matter.

∾

The refutation of suicide: is it not inelegant to abandon a world which has so willingly put itself at the service of our melancholy?

∾

However patiently one intoxicates oneself, impossible to achieve the assurance of that asylum-Croesus who said: "To be at peace, I have bought myself all air, and made it my personal property."

∾

Our embarrassment in the presence of a ridiculous man derives from the fact that we cannot imagine him on his deathbed.

~

Only optimists commit suicide, the optimists who can no longer be . . . optimists. The others, having no reason to live, why should they have any to die?

~

Bilious minds? Those who revenge themselves on their thoughts for the gaiety they lavish on their transactions with others.

~

I knew nothing about her; our encounter nonetheless took the most macabre turn: I spoke to her of the sea, of a certain commentary on Ecclesiastes. And imagine my stupefaction when, after my tirade on the hysteria of the waves, she produced this remark: "Self-pity is not a good thing."

~

Woe to the unbeliever who, confronting his insomnias, possesses only a limited stock of prayers!

~

Is it no more than chance that all those who broadened my views of death were society's dregs?

~

For the madman, any scapegoat will do. He endures his defeats as an accuser; objects striking him as culpable as human beings, he assaults whatever and whomever he pleases; delirium is an expanding economy; — limited to larger discriminations, we fall back on our defeats, we cling to them, failing to find their cause or their sustenance outside ourselves; common sense compels us to a closed economy, to the autarky of failure.

~

"It ill becomes you," you informed me, "to keep pestiferating against the order of things."
"Can I help it if I am only a parvenu of neurosis, a Job in search of a leprosy, a trumpery Buddha, a lost and lazy Scyth?"

~

Sighs and satires seem to me equally valid. Whether I read a lampoon or an *ars moriendi*, everything there is true . . . With the unconstraint of pity, I pore over the truths and identify myself with the words.

"Thou shalt be objective!" — curse of the nihilist who *believes in everything!*

~

At the apogee of our disgusts, a rat seems to have crept into our brain to dream there.

~

It is not the precepts of Stoicism which will show us the utility of affronts or the seduction of catastrophes. The manuals of insensibility are all too reasonable. But if each man were to make his little experiment as a bum! To dress in rags, post yourself at the crossroads, to extend your palm to the passersby, to suffer their contempt or thank them for their coin — now there's a discipline! Or to venture into the street and insult strangers, to endure their beatings . . .

For a long time I frequented courtrooms solely to contemplate habitual criminals, their superiority to the laws, their readiness for ruin. And yet they are pitiful compared to the whores, to the ease those women show in the dock. So much detachment is . . . disconcerting; no *amour-propre* whatever; insults draw no blood; no adjective is wounding. Their cynicism is the form of their honesty. A girl of seventeen, majestically frightful, replies to the judge trying to wrest a promise to keep off the sidewalks: "I can't promise you that, Your Honor."

One measures one's own strength only in humiliation. In order to console ourselves for the shames we have not known, we would have to inflict them upon ourselves, spit in the mirror, waiting for the public to honor us with its saliva. God preserve us from a *distinguished* fate!

~

I have so fondled the notion of fatality, nourished it at the cost of such great sacrifices, that it has finally made itself incarnate: once an abstraction, here it is, palpitating before me and crushing me with all the life I have given it.

Religion

If I believed in God, my fatuousness would be limitless; I would walk naked in the streets . . .

~

So utterly have the saints resorted to the facility of paradox that it is impossible not to cite them in the salons.

~

When one is devoured by such an appetite for suffering that to satisfy it would take thousands of existences, we realize out of what hell must have arisen the notion of transmigration.

~

Outside of matter, all is music; God Himself is merely a sonorous hallucination.

∾

Pursuing the antecedents of a sigh can lead us to the moment before — as to the sixth day of Creation.

∾

The organ is the one instrument that makes us understand how eternity can *develop*.

∾

Those nights when one can advance no further toward God, when one has traversed Him in all directions, when one has worn Him out with trampling — those nights from which one emerges with the notion of casting Him on the junk heap . . . , of enriching the world with one more piece of rubbish.

∾

Without the vigilance of irony, how easy it would be to found a religion! Merely allow the gawkers to collect around our loquacious trances.

~

It is not God, it is Grief which enjoys the advantages of ubiquity.

~

In the crucial ordeals, a cigarette is more effective help than the Gospels.

~

Suso tells how he took a stylet and cut the name of Jesus into his flesh, right above his heart. He did not bleed in vain: sometime afterward, a light emanated from his wound.

Had I a greater faith in my incredulity, could I not, inscribing another name in my flesh, the name of the Adversary, serve him as a luminous sign!

~

I sought a standing in Time; it was uninhabitable. When I turned to Eternity, I lost my footing altogether.

~

A moment comes when each man says to himself, "Either God or me," and engages in a combat from which both emerge diminished.

~

A man's secret coincides with the sufferings he craves.

~

Knowing no more, with regard to religious experience, than the qualms of erudition, the moderns *weigh* the Absolute, study its varieties, and save their thrills for myths — those intoxications of an historical consciousness. Having ceased praying, we find fault with prayer. No more exclamations; nothing but theories. Religion boycotts faith. In the past, with love or hatred, we ventured into God, Who, from the inexhaustible Nothing He once was, is now — to the great despair of mystics and atheists — no more than a *problem*.

~

Like every iconoclast, I have broken my idols in order to offer sacrifices to their debris.

~

94

What is the source of our obsession with the Reptile? — Might it not be our terror of a last temptation, of an imminent and, this time, irreparable Fall, which would make us lose even the *memory* of Paradise?

∾

Those days when, getting out of bed, my ears filled with a funeral march, I would hum all day long until, by evening, it vanished, quite spent, into an *anthem* . . .

∾

How great is Christianity's guilt for having corrupted skepticism! A Greek would never have associated lamentation with doubt. He would recoil horror-struck before a Pascal, and even more before that inflation of the soul which, ever since the cross, has demonized the mind.

∾

To be more unserviceable than a saint . . .

∾

In our nostalgia for death, so great a flaccidity descends upon us, such a modification occurs in our veins, that we forget about death and ponder nothing but the chemistry of the blood.

~

The Creation was the first act of sabotage.

~

The unbeliever debauched by the Abyss and enraged at being unable to wrest himself from it deploys a mystical zeal in constructing a world as devoid of depth as a ballet by Rameau.

~

The Old Testament knew how to intimidate Heaven, how to shake a fist at whatever was on high: prayer was a quarrel between the creature and its creator. Came the Gospels to make nice: Christianity's unforgivable error.

~

That which lives without memory has not left Paradise: the plants still delight in it. They were not doomed to Sin, to that impossibility of *forgetting;* but we, cases of walking remorse, etc., etc.

(To regret Paradise! — One could scarcely be more out of it nor take further the passion for desuetude or provincialism.)

∾

"Lord, without Thee I am mad, yet with Thee madder still!" — Such would be, in the best of cases, the result of a resumption of contact between the failure here below and the failure on high.

∾

The great mistake of suffering is to have *organized* Chaos, to have reduced it to a universe.

∾

What a temptation the churches, if there were no faithful in them but only those tensions of God the organ tells us of!

∾

When I graze the Mystery without being able to mock it, I wonder what is the use of lucidity, that vaccine against the Absolute.

∾

What a fuss over setting oneself up in the desert! More cunning than those first hermits, we have learned to seek it in ourselves.

~

It is as an informer that I have prowled around God; incapable of imploring Him, I have spied on Him.

~

For two thousand years, Jesus has revenged himself on us for not having died on a sofa.

~

Dilettantes take no notice of God; madmen and drunkards, those great specialists, make Him the object of their ruminations.

It is to a saving remnant of judgment that we owe the privilege of being still superficial.

~

To eliminate from oneself the toxins of time in order to retain those of eternity — such is the mystic's child's play.

~

The possibility of self-renewal by heresy confers upon the believer a distinct superiority over the atheist.

～

One is never lower than when one regrets the angels . . . unless it is when one longs to pray to the point of cerebral liquefaction.

～

Even more than religion, cynicism commits the error of granting man too much attention.

～

Between God and the French, guile intervenes.

～

As is only fair, I itemized the arguments favorable to God; His inexistence seemed to me to emerge intact. He has the genius of calling Himself into question by all His works; His defenders render Him odious; His worshipers, suspect. If you fear loving Him, you need merely open your Aquinas . . .

And I think of that Central European theology professor questioning one of his students about the proofs of the existence of God: she goes through the historical argument, the ontological, etc. But she is careful to add: "All the same I don't believe in Him." The professor is annoyed, takes up the proofs again, one by one; she shrugs and persists in her incredulity. Then the master draws himself up to his full height, *scarlet* with faith: "Young lady, I give you my word of honor that He exists!"

. . . An argument in itself worth all the theological Summae.

What are we to say about Immortality? To seek to elucidate it, or simply to approach it, is either aberration or fraud. Treatises nonetheless reveal its impossible fascination. If we are to believe them, we have only to entrust ourselves to a few deductions hostile to Time . . . And there we are, furnished with eternity, indemnified against the dust, exempt from agony.

It is not these trifles which have made me doubt my fragility. How much, on the other hand, I've been troubled by the meditations of an old friend, a somewhat unhinged itinerant musician! Like all lunatics, he is beset with the problems he puts to himself: he has "solved" any number. That

day, after he had made his rounds of the café ter-
races, he came to question me about . . . immortality. "It's unthinkable," I told him, at once
seduced and repelled by his timeless eyes, his
wrinkles, his rags. A certainty inspired him:
"You're mistaken not to believe in it; if you don't
believe in it, you won't survive. I'm sure that death
will have no power over me. Moreover, whatever
you say, everything has a soul. There! did you see
the birds flying about in the streets, then suddenly
rising above the houses to *look* at Paris? There's a
soul there, such things cannot die!"

~

In order to regain its ascendancy over
men's minds, Catholicism requires a raging pope,
gnawed by contradictions, a dispenser of hysteria,
dominated by heretic frenzy, a barbarian unem-
barrassed by two thousand years of theology. —
In Rome and in the rest of Christendom have
demential resources utterly dried up? Since the
end of the sixteenth century, the church, human-
ized, has produced no more than second-rate
schisms, mediocre saints, laughable excommuni-
cations. And if a madman did not manage to save
her, at least he would cast her into a *superior* abyss.

~

Of all that theologians have conceived, the only readable pages and the only true utterances are those devoted to the Adversary. How greatly their tone alters, their verve quickens when they turn their back on the Light in order to attend to the Darkness! As if they were climbing back down into their element, which they are rediscovering. At last they can hate, they are authorized to do so: no more sublime purring, no more edifying repetitions. Hatred can be vile; yet to rid oneself of hatred is more dangerous than to abuse it. The Church, in its high wisdom, has spared its own such risks; in order to satisfy their instincts, it excites them against the Evil One; they cling to him, nibble him: fortunately, an inexhaustible bone . . . If we were to take it from them, they would succumb to vice or to apathy.

~

Even when we believe we have dislodged God from our soul, He still lingers: we realize that He finds it tedious there, but we no longer have sufficient faith to entertain Him . . .

~

Why should I lay down my arms? — I have not experienced all the contradictions, I still have the hope of a new *impasse*.

❧

How many years now that I've been dechristianizing myself *as far as the eye can see!*

❧

All belief makes us insolent; newly acquired, it inspires the worst instincts; people who do not share it appear either impotent or vanquished, deserving only pity and scorn. Consider the neophytes in politics and especially in religion, all those who have managed to interest God in their arrangements, the converts, the *nouveaux riches* of the Absolute. Compare their impertinence with the modesty and the good manners of those who are in the process of losing their faith and their convictions . . .

❧

On the frontiers of the self: "What I have suffered, what I am suffering, no one will ever know, not even I."

❧

When, out of the appetite for solitude, we have sundered our bonds, the Void seizes us: nothing, no one . . . Whom to liquidate now? Where to unearth a durable victim? — Such perplexities open us to God: at least with Him we're sure of being able to *break* indefinitely . . .

Love's Vitality

Only erotic natures sacrifice to boredom, disappointed in advance by love.

~

Losing love is so rich a philosophical ordeal that it makes a hairdresser into a rival of Socrates.

~

The art of love? Being able to unite the discretion of an anemone with the temperament of a vampire.

~

In the pursuit of torment, the search for suffering, only a jealous man can rival a martyr. Yet we canonize the latter and ridicule the former.

～

Why the marriage hearse? Why not the hearse of love? — So regrettable, Blake's restriction.

～

Onan, Sade, Masoch — what luck they had! Their names, like their exploits, will never date.

～

Love's Vitality: one can hardly disparage a sentiment which has survived both romanticism and the bidet.

～

The lover who kills himself for a girl has an experience which is more complete and much more profound than the hero who overturns the world.

～

Who would wear himself out in the grip of sexuality unless he hoped to lose his reason for a little over a second, for the rest of his days?

~

Sometimes I dream of a remote and vaporous love like the schizophrenia of a perfume.

~

To feel one's brain: a phenomenon equally deadly to thought and to virility.

~

He buries his forehead between her breasts, between two continents of Death ...

~

A monk and a butcher fight it out within each desire.

~

Only simulated passions, the fake ecstasies have some relation to the mind, to our self-respect; sincere feelings presuppose a lack of consideration . . . for oneself.

∾

Happy in love, Adam would have spared us History.

∾

I've always thought Diogenes must have suffered some misfortune in love when he was young: one does not take the path of derision without the help of a venereal disease or an intractable chambermaid.

∾

Some performances one pardons only when they are one's own: if we envisaged others at the climax of a certain spasm, it would be impossible to shake their hands again.

∾

The flesh is incompatible with charity: orgasm transforms the saint into a wolf.

∾

After metaphors, the drugstore. — Which is how the grandest sentiments disintegrate.

To begin as a poet and to end as a gynecologist! Surely being a lover is the least enviable of all conditions.

～

One declares war on the glands and prostrates oneself at the first whiff of the first mistress . . . What use is pride against the liturgy of odors, against a zoological incense?

～

To conceive a love chaster than a springtime, a love which — depressed by the fornication of flowers — would weep at their roots.

～

I can understand and justify all the anomalies, in love and elsewhere; but that among fools some should be impotent — that is beyond me.

～

Sexuality: surgery and ashes, Balkanization of bodies, bestiality of a back-number saint, racket of a risible and unforgettable collapse . . .

～

In pleasure, as in panic, we reinstate our origins; the ape, unfairly relegated, at last achieves glory — for the space of a cry.

～

A breath of irony in sex perverts its function and changes its practitioner into a Species fraud.

～

Two needy victims, amazed at their torment, at their noisy sudation. To what ritual are we compelled by the gravity of the senses and the body's solemnity.

To burst out laughing in the spasm itself — sole means of defying the prescriptions of the blood, the body's grim rites.

～

Hasn't everyone endured the confessions of some poor wretch, compared to whom Tristan would sound like a pimp?

~

Love's dignity resides in the disabused affection surviving a moment's slobber.

~

If the impotent only knew how considerate of them nature had been, they would bless their glands' somnolence and boast of it on every street corner.

~

Ever since Schopenhauer had the preposterous inspiration of introducing sexuality into metaphysics, and Freud that of supplanting licentiousness by a pseudoscience of our confusions, it is only to be expected that the first-comer should beguile us with the "meaning" of his exploits, his timidities, and his successes. All confidences begin here; here all conversations end. Soon our relations with others will come down to the record of their effective or invented orgasms . . . It is the fate

111

of our race, devastated by introspection and anemia, to reproduce itself in words, to flaunt its
nights and puff their triumphs and tribulations.

∿

The more disabused a man's mind, the
more he risks, stricken by love, reacting like a
schoolgirl.

∿

Two paths lie open to man and to woman:
ferocity or indifference. Everything suggests that
they will take the second, that there will be,
between them, neither explanation nor rupture
but that they will continue to move further and
further apart; that pederasty and onanism, sug-
gested by the schools and the churches, will win
over the masses; that any number of abolished
vices will be restored to power; and that scientific
procedures will compensate for the inefficiency of
the spasm and the malediction of the couple.

∿

A mixture of anatomy and ecstasy, apothe-
osis of the insoluble, ideal nourishment for the

bulimia of disappointment, Love leads us toward
the lower depths of glory . . .

~

We always love . . . despite; and that
"despite" covers an infinity.

On Music

Born with an habitual soul, I sought one of another sort from music: this was the start of unhoped-for misfortunes . . .

~

Suppose that music, lacking the imperialism of the Concept, had taken the place of philosophy: the paradise of inexpressible evidence, an epidemic of ecstasies.

~

Beethoven vitiated music: introducing fits of temper, granting admission to *anger.*

~

Without Bach, Theology would be devoid of an object, Creation would be fictive, and Nothingness peremptory.

If there is anyone who owes everything to Bach, it is certainly God.

～

What's the use of frequenting Plato, when a saxophone can just as well offer a glimpse of another world?

～

Defenseless against music, I must submit to its despotism and, depending on its whim, be god or garbage.

～

There was a time when, unable to conceive of an eternity which would have separated me from Mozart, I no longer feared death. This happened with each musician, with all music . . .

～

Chopin elevated the piano to the status of phthisis.

～

The universe of sound: onomatopoeia of the inexpressible, enigma displayed, infinity perceived, and ineffable . . . Upon experiencing its seduction, one's only plan is to be embalmed within a sigh.

~

Music is the refuge of souls wounded by happiness.

~

The only true music is the music which makes us *palpate* time.

~

Immediate infinity, a meaningless expression for philosophy, is the reality, the very essence of music.

~

Had I yielded to music's lures and flatteries, to all the worlds it has created and destroyed within me, I should long since, out of pride, have lost my reason.

~

117

The North's aspiration toward a *different sky* has engendered German music — geometry of autumns, alcohol of concepts, metaphysical intoxication.

Nineteenth-century Italy — that bazaar of sounds — lacked the dimension of night, the art of crushing shadows to extract their essence.

One must side with Brahms or with the sun.

~

Music, a system of farewells, evokes a physics whose point of departure is not atoms but tears.

~

Perhaps I have staked too much on music, perhaps I have not taken all my precautions against the acrobatics of the sublime, against the charlatanism of the Ineffable . . .

~

Certain of Mozart's andantes give off an ethereal desolation, a sort of dream funeral in another life.

~

When music itself is helpless to save us, a dagger gleams before our eyes; nothing sustains us except perhaps the fascination of crime.

~

How gladly I'd die by music, as punishment for having occasionally doubted the sovereignty of its bedevilments!

Vertigo of History

When it first experimented with disaster, no one would have believed an undeveloped humanity capable of mass-producing *a day*.

~

Had Noah possessed the gift of foreseeing the future, there is not a doubt in the world he would have scuttled the ark.

~

History's trepidation belongs to psychiatry, as indeed do all the motives of action: to move is to defect from reason, is to risk the strait jacket.

~

Events — tumors of Time.

~

Evolution: Prometheus, nowadays, would be an elected member of the opposition party.

~

The hour of crime does not sound at the same time for all peoples. Hence, the permanence of history.

~

Each man's ambition is to plumb the Worst, to be the perfect prophet. Alas! there are so many catastrophes which have never crossed our minds!

~

Contrary to the other centuries, which practiced torture negligently, ours, more exigent in the matter, exerts a purist's conscientiousness which does honor to our cruelty.

~

All indignation — from grousing to satanism — marks a point in mental evolution.

~

Freedom is the supreme good only for those animated by the *will* to heresy.

~

How vague it is to say: I tend toward one system rather than another. It would be more exact to acknowledge: I prefer this police state to that one. History, indeed, comes down to a classi-fication of police; for what does the historian deal with if not men's conception of the *gendarme* through the ages?

~

No longer speak of enslaved peoples nor of their craving for freedom; the tyrants are assassi-nated too late: that is their great excuse.

~

In periods of peace, hating for the pleasure of hating, we must find the enemies which suit us; — a delicious task which exciting times spare us.

∿

Man *secretes* disaster.

∿

I love those nations of astronomers: Chaldeans, Assyrians, pre-Columbians who, for love of the sky, went bankrupt in history.

∿

An authentically chosen people, the Gypsies bear the responsibility for no event, for no institution. They have triumphed over the earth by their desire to *found* nothing upon it.

∿

A few more generations and laughter, reserved to the initiate, will be as impracticable as ecstasy.

∿

A nation dies out when it no longer reacts to fanfares: Decadence is the death of the bugle.

~

Skepticism is the stimulant of young civilizations and the prudence of old ones.

~

Mental therapeutics abound among rich nations: the absence of *immediate* anxieties sustains a sickly climate. In order to preserve its nervous well-being, a nation needs a substantial disaster, an *object* for its afflictions, a positive terror justifying its "complexes." Societies consolidate in danger and atrophy in neutrality. Where peace and hygiene and comfort flourish, psychoses multiply.

...I come from a country which, never having known happiness, has produced but one psychoanalyst.

~

Tyrants, their ferocity slaked, become meek; everything would work out if the jealous slaves did not insist, they too, on slaking theirs.

The lamb's aspiration to become a wolf brings about the majority of events. Those who have none dream of fangs; they would devour in their turn and succeed in doing so by the bestiality of numbers.

History — *that dynamism of victims.*

~

For having classed intelligence among the virtues and stupidity among the vices, France has enlarged the realm of morality. Whence her advantage over the other nations, her vaporous supremacy.

~

We might measure the degree of a civilization's refinement by the number of liver sufferers, of impotent men or neurotic women. — But why confine ourselves to these deficient types when there are so many others who attest, by the failure of their viscera or of their glands, to the Mind's fatal prosperity?

~

The biologically weak, finding no satisfaction in life, go about changing its *données.*

Why weren't the reformers isolated at the first *symptoms* of faith? and why was there any delay in consigning them to a hospital or a prison? At twelve years of age, the Galilean should have had his place there. Society is poorly organized: it takes no action against the delirious who don't die young.

~

Skepticism spreads its blessings upon us too late, upon our faces deteriorated by our convictions, upon our faces of hyenas with an ideal.

~

A book on war — Clausewitz's — was Lenin's pillow book and Hitler's. — And we still wonder why this century is doomed!

~

To make our way from the caves to the salons required a considerable amount of time; will we take as long to cover the path back, or will we take shortcuts? — An idle question for those who have no *presentiment* of prehistory . . .

~

All calamities — revolutions, wars, persecutions — derive from an *almost* inscribed on a flag.

~

Only the failed nations approach a "human" ideal; the others, those who succeed, bear the stigmata of their glory, of their gilded bestiality.

~

In our fear, we are victims of an *aggression* of the Future.

~

A statesman who shows no sign of senility is the one I am afraid of.

~

The great nations, having the initiative of their miseries, can vary them at will; the minor ones are reduced to those which are imposed upon them.

~

Anxiety — or the fanaticism of the worst.

~

When the mob espouses a myth, expect a massacre or, worse still, a new religion.

~

Violent actions are the appanage of the nations which, alien to the pleasure of lingering at table, are ignorant of the poetry of dessert and the melancholies of digestion.

~

Without its assiduity to the ridiculous, would the human race have lasted more than a single generation?

~

There is more honesty and rigor in the occult sciences than in the philosophies which assign a "meaning" to history.

~

This century carries me back to the dawn of time, to the last days of Chaos. I hear the groans of matter; the calls of the Inanimate echo through space; my bones sink into the prehistoric, while my blood flows in the veins of the first reptiles.

∼

The merest glance at the itinerary of civilization gives me the presumption of Cassandra.

∼

Man's "liberation"? — It will come the day when, rid of his finalist tendency, he will have understood the accidental nature of his advent and the gratuitousness of his ordeals, where each will shudder as a learned and nimble victim and where, for the populace itself, "life" will be reduced to its just proportions, to an *hypothesis of labor.*

∼

Not until you've seen a brothel at five in the morning can you realize toward what lethargies our planet is making its way.

∼

History is *indefensible.* You must react to it with the cynic's inflexible abulia; either you side with the masses or you walk with the mob of rebels, murderers, and believers.

~

Has Man-the-Experiment failed? It had already failed with Adam. Yet one question is justified: will we be inventive enough to appear as innovators, to *add* to that failure?

Meanwhile, let us persevere in the mistake of being men, let us behave as jokers of the Fall, let us be *terribly* light!

~

Nothing consoles me for not having known the moment when earth broke with the sun — unless it is the prospect of knowing the one when men break with the earth.

~

Formerly, people shifted gravely from one contradiction to the next; nowadays we experience so many at once that we no longer know which to cling to, which to resolve.

~

Impenitent rationalists, incapable of accommodating ourselves to Fate or of perceiving its meaning, we regard ourselves as the center of our actions and believe we collapse of *our own free will.* Let one crucial experience intervene in our life, and destiny, once so imprecise and abstract, acquires in our eyes the prestige of a sensation. So each in his own way makes his entrance into the Irrational.

~

A civilization at the end of its trajectory, fortunate anomaly that it was, withers into conformity, models itself on the mediocre nations, wallows in failure, and converts its fate into a unique problem. Of this self-obsession, Spain provides the perfect example. After having known, in the days of the Conquistadors, a bestial superhumanity, she has given herself over to ruminating upon her past, repeating her lacunae, letting her virtues and her genius gather mildew; on the other hand, in love with her own decline, she has adopted it as a new supremacy. How could we fail to perceive that such historical masochism has ceased to be a Spanish singularity and become the climate and indeed the code of a continent's downfall.

~

Today, on the theme of the senility of civilizations, any illiterate could rival *shudders* with Gibbon, Nietzsche, or Spengler.

∽

The end of history, the end of man? Can it be a serious matter to ponder such things? — These are remote events which Anxiety — greedy for *imminent* disasters — seeks to precipitate at all costs.

Where the Void Begins

I believe in the salvation of humanity, in the future of cyanide . . .

~

Will man ever recover from the mortal blow he has delivered to life?

~

I cannot reconcile myself with things, were each moment to wrest itself out of time to give me a kiss.

~

He is merely a mind crannied to have openings onto the beyond.

～

Who, in pitch-darkness, looking into a mirror, has not seen projected there the crimes which *await him?*

～

If we had the faculty of exaggerating our evils, it would be impossible for us to endure them. By attributing unwonted proportions to them, we consider ourselves chosen reprobates, elect in reverse, flattered and stimulated by disgrace.

For our greater good, there exists in each of us a braggart of the Incurable.

～

Everything must be revised, even sobs . . .

～

When Aeschylus or Tacitus seems tepid, open a Life of the Insects — a revelation of rage and futility, an inferno which, fortunately for us, will have neither a playwright nor a chronicler. What would remain of our tragedies if a literate bug were to offer us his?

∾

You do not act, yet you resent the fever of high deeds; without enemies, you wage an exhausting battle . . . This is the *gratuitous tension* of neurosis, which would give even a grocer the shudders of a defeated general.

∾

I cannot contemplate a smile without reading in it: "Look at me! it's for the last time."

∾

Lord, take pity on my blood, on my anemia in flames!

∾

How much concentration, industry, and tact it takes to destroy our *raison d'être!*

∾

When I realize that individuals are merely life stammering, and that life itself isn't worth much more with regard to matter, I make for the first bistro with the notion of never coming out. And yet were I to drain a thousand bottles in there, they could never give me the taste for Utopia, for that belief that something is still possible.

～

Each of us shuts himself up in his fear — his ivory tower.

～

The secret of my adaptation to life? — I've changed despairs the way I've changed shirts.

～

In each blackout, we feel a kind of final sensation — in God.

～

My greed for agonies has made me die so many times that it strikes me as indecent to keep on abusing a corpse from which I can get nothing more.

～

Why Being or some other capitalized word? God *sounded* better. We ought to have kept that one. After all, shouldn't reasons of euphony regulate truth-functions?

~

In the state of paroxysm without cause, fatigue is a delirium, and the fatigued person the demiurge of a sub-universe.

~

Each day is a Rubicon in which I aspire to be drowned.

~

No founder of a religion displays a pity comparable to what we find in one of Pierre Janet's patients. She would have crying jags on the subject, among others, of "that poor Department of Seine-et-Oise which encloses and contains the Department of the Seine without ever being able to get rid of it."

In pity, as in everything, the madhouse has the last word.

~

In our dreams surfaces the madman within; having ruled our nights, he falls asleep in the depths of ourselves, at the heart of the Species; yet sometimes we hear him snoring in our thoughts . . .

~

Who trembles for his depression, who dreads recovering from it — how relieved he is to observe that his fears are ill founded, that it is incurable!

~

"Where do you get those superior airs of yours?"
"I've managed to survive, you see, all those nights when I wondered: am I going to kill myself at dawn?"

~

The moment we believe we've understood *everything* grants us the look of a murderer.

~

We emerge into the irrevocable only from the moment we can no longer renew our regrets.

∾

Those ideas which soar above space itself and which, all of a sudden, bump into the walls of the skull . . .

∾

A religious nature is defined less by its convictions than by the need to prolong its sufferings beyond death.

∾

I observe, in terror, the diminution of my hatred of mankind, the loosening of the last link uniting me with it.

∾

Insomnia is the only form of heroism compatible with the bed.

∾

Young and ambitious, you will suffer no greater misfortune than to consort with those who know men. I've frequented three or four such: they *did me in* at twenty.

~

The Truth? It is in Shakespeare; — a philosopher cannot appropriate it without exploding along with his system.

~

When we have exhausted the pretexts which incite us to gaiety or melancholy, we come to the point of experiencing either one *in a pure state:* which is how we join the mad . . .

~

After having so often exposed the *folie des grandeurs* in others, how could I without absurdity still believe myself to be the most ineffective man in the world, first in the ranks of the useless?

~

"A single thought addressed to God is worth more than the universe" (Katherina Emmerich). — How right she is, poor saint...

~

Madness is achieved only by the garrulous and the taciturn: those who have emptied themselves of all mystery and those who have accumulated too much.

~

In dread — that megalomania in reverse — we become the center of a universal whirlwind, while the stars pirouette around us.

~

When an idea is sufficiently ripe on the Tree of Knowledge, what ecstasy to insinuate oneself there, to function as a grub, and to hasten its fall!

~

In order not to insult others' labor or their beliefs, so as not to be accused of either apathy or sloth, I have flung myself into Confusion until it became my form of piety.

~

The inclination to suicide is characteristic of timorous murderers, those who respect the laws; fearful of killing, they dream of wiping themselves out, sure as they are of impunity.

~

"When I shave," this half-mad man once told me, "who if not God keeps me from cutting my own throat?" — Faith, in other words, would be no more than an artifice of the instinct of self-preservation. Biology everywhere.

~

It is out of *fear of suffering* that we struggle so to abolish reality. Our efforts crowned with success, such abolition reveals itself as a source of sufferings.

~

If you don't see death *en rose*, you are suffering from color blindness of the heart.

~

Not having managed to celebrate abortion or legalize cannibalism, modern societies must resolve their difficulties by prompter methods.

~

The last resort of those stricken by fate is the *idea* of fate.

~

How I'd like to be a plant, even if I had to keep vigil over a piece of shit!

~

That mob of ancestors lamenting in my blood... Out of respect for their defeats, I demean myself to sighs.

~

Everything persecutes our ideas, beginning with our brain.

~

We can't know whether man will long continue to make use of words or gradually recover the *use* of screaming.

~

Paris, remotest point from Paradise, remains nonetheless the only site where it feels good to despair.

~

Some souls God Himself could not save were He to kneel and pray for them.

~

A sick man once told me: "What use are my pains? I'm no poet able to turn them to use or to the satisfactions of vanity."

~

When, the motives of revolt being liquidated, we no longer know against what to rebel, we experience a vertigo such that we would give our lives in exchange for just one prejudice.

~

When we turn pale, our blood withdraws in order no longer to interpose between us and who knows what . . .

～

To each his own . . . madness: mine was to suppose myself normal, dangerously normal. And since others seemed mad to me, I ended by being afraid, afraid of them and, even more, afraid of myself.

～

After certain fits of eternity and of fever, we wonder why we have not deigned to be God.

～

The meditative and the carnal: Pascal and Tolstoy. To feel for death or to abhor it, to discover it by the mind or by physiology. — With undermined instincts, Pascal surmounts his dreads, whereas Tolstoy, outraged by dying, reminds us of a haggard elephant, a flattened jungle. One no longer meditates at the *equators of the blood.*

～

The man who, by successive inadvertences, has neglected to kill himself seems to himself no more and no less than a veteran of pain, a pensioner of suicide.

≈

The more intimate I become with certain twilights, the surer I am that the only ones to have understood something of our horde are cabaret singers, quacks, and madmen.

≈

To attenuate our pangs, to convert them into *doubts* — a stratagem inspired in us by cowardice, that skepticism for universal use.

≈

Involuntary access to ourselves, sickness compels us, condemns us to "profundity." The invalid? A metaphysician in spite of himself.

≈

After having vainly sought a country of adoption, to fall back on death, in order, in such new exile, to set up as a *citizen*.

≈

Any being who *manifests* himself rejuvenates in his fashion original sin.

❧

Retreating to the drama of the glands, attentive to the confidences of the mucous membrane, Disgust makes us all physiologists.

❧

If it weren't for blood's insipid taste, the ascetic would define himself by his refusal to be a vampire.

❧

The spermatozoon is the bandit in a pure state.

❧

To stockpile fatalities, to flounder between catechisms and orgies, to wallow in the distraction, and — besotted nomad — to model oneself on God, that stateless exile . . .

❧

Not knowing humiliation, you are ignorant of what it is to arrive at the last stage of yourself.

~

My doubts I have acquired painfully; my disappointments, as if they had always been *waiting for me*, came of their own accord — primordial illuminations.

~

On a globe composing its own epitaph, let us have enough decorum to behave as *nice corpses*.

~

Like it or not, we are all psychoanalysts, amateurs of the mysteries of the heart and the undies, deep-sea divers into horrors. Woe to the mind with a transparent abyss!

~

In sloth, we slide toward the nadir of the soul and of space, toward the antipodes of ecstasy, where the Void begins.

~

The more we frequent men, the blacker our thoughts; and when, to clarify them, we return to our solitude, we find there the shadow they have cast.

~

Disabused wisdom must hark back to some geological era: the dinosaurs may have died of it . . .

~

When I was barely adolescent, the prospect of death flung me into trances; to escape them, I rushed to the brothel, where I invoked the angels. But with age, you become used to your own terrors, you undertake nothing more in order to be disengaged from them, you become quite bourgeois in the Abyss. — And although there was a time when I envied those Egyptian monks who dug their own graves in order to shed tears within them, if I were to dig mine now, all I would drop in there would be cigarette butts.